CYRUS L DAY

knots &
splices

SECOND EDITION

REVISED AND PHOTOGRAPHED BY
COLIN JARMAN

new
7/06

International Marine / McGraw-Hill

Camden, Maine • New York • Chicago • San Francisco • Lisbon
Mexico City • Milan • New Delhi • San Juan • Seoul • Singapore

623.888
J

Published by International Marine/McGraw-Hill
www.internationalmarine.com

Copyright First edition © Cyrus L Day 1953
Copyright Second edition © Cyrus L Day and Colin Jarman 2006
Copyright Second edition photos © Colin Jarman 2006

First published 1953
Reprinted 1954, 1957, 1960, 1962, 1970, 1975, 1976, 1977,
1978, 1981, 1982, 1983, 1985, 1987, 1988, 1991, 1996, 1998
Revised 2001
Reprinted 2004
Second edition 2006

ISBN 0-07-147466-8

A CIP catalog record for this book is available from the Library of Congress.

Questions regarding the ordering of this book should be addressed to
The McGraw-Hill Companies
Customer Service Department
P.O. Box 547
Blacklick, OH 43004
Retail customers: 1-800-262-4729
Bookstores: 1-800-722-4726

Typeset in 8 on 10pt FF Din Regular
Printed and Bound by Star Standard Pte Ltd, Singapore.

All ropes' ends shown in this book are finished with tape rather than a whipping
in order to make them clearly visible within the pictures and to help readers follow
the pattern of the knots.

CONTENTS

FOREWORD TO THE 2ND EDITION

Knots & Splices has been in print for over 50 years, which must stand as quite a record for a book of this type. A copy was given to me as a Christmas present around 1957 and it sparked an interest in knots and rope work that has lasted to this day. The knots and splices I learned from Cyrus Day have stood me in good stead over a lifetime of boating, and it was with huge excitement that I took on the project of updating this book for the 21st century. I hope that he would have approved of what I've done to his book; I hope it will inspire others as his did me and that it will continue in print for another 50 years!

Colin Jarman

DEDICATION

To Cyrus L Day who awoke my interest in knots and ropework.

ACKNOWLEDGEMENT

The author would like to thank Bainbridge International for supplying Robline Rope to use in the photographs.

NOTE

All ropes' ends shown in this book are finished with tape rather than a whipping in order to make them clearly visible within the pictures and help readers to follow the pattern of the knots.

GLOSSARY

BELAY
To make a line fast on a cleat, pin, pair of bitts or the like.

BEND
(Noun) A knot used to tie the ends of two free lines together. **(Verb)** To make fast or to tie, as in 'to bend two lines together'.

BIGHT
(1) The middle of a line, **(2)** a loop or curve in a line.

BITT
A vertical timber or metal post set in the deck for securing hawsers and other lines.

BLOCK
A roller or sheave that rotates on a pin or ball race held between two metal or plastic cheeks. The sheave either spins on a simple pin (like a wheel on an axle) or on a set of ball bearings (known as a ball race) around a pin.

CLEAT
(Noun) A shaped piece of wood, metal or plastic with two arms or horns on which to belay a line. **(Verb)** To belay a line to a cleat.

HAWSER
A heavy rope used for towing.

HEAT SEAL
To heat the ends of synthetic rope by means of a heated cutter or naked flame to melt and fuse the strands to prevent fraying.

HITCH
A knot used to secure a line to a spar, ring, post or the like.

KNOT
In general, **(1)** any fastening, including bends and hitches, made by interweaving cordage. Specifically, **(2)** a method of joining the ends of a single line together or of forming **(3)** a noose, **(4)** a fixed loop or **(5)** a stopper in the end of a rope.

LAY	**(Noun)** The direction in which the strands of a rope are twisted or plaited together. **(Verb)** To twist the strands of a rope together. (To unlay is to separate the strands.)
LINE	A rope used for a particular purpose.
MARL	To bind or secure with a series of Marling Hitches (see page 56).
MARLINE SPIKE	A pointed implement for opening the lay of a rope when splicing.
MOORING WARP	A line specifically for securing vessels to a quay, dock, pontoon or slip.
NOOSE	A knot with a loop that slides and tightens under load.
RATLINES	Horizontal lines fastened between shrouds to form a ladder by which to climb aloft.
REEF POINTS	Lengths of rope fixed in a sail at regular intervals along a reef band and used in reefing (shortening sail).
RIDING TURN	Commonly, when one turn of a sheet rides over another on the barrel of the sheet winch and jams.
RODE	Anchor cable. May be chain or chain and rope.
ROPE	Cordage of more than 5-6mm diameter. It may be laid up as a three-strand twist, plaited as a multiplait of eight strands, formed with a laid or braided core inside a braided sheath and several other structures.
SEIZING	A lashing for holding two spars, two ropes or two parts of the same rope tightly together.
SERVE	To bind, much like seizing, but around a single rope.
SHEAVE	The grooved roller in a block.

SHEET	A strop or loop for hoisting and lowering a person or a load.
SLING	A rope used to control the angle of the sail to the wind.
STANDING PART	The main part of a rope or line, as distinct from a bight, a loop or an end.
STOP	To lash or seize temporarily using light line or cord.
STOPPER KNOT	A knot to prevent a rope or line from running out through an eye or a block.
STRAND	A bundle of fibres or yarns from which a rope is made.
STROP	A sling or loop for raising and lowering objects.
THIMBLE	A grooved piece of metal or plastic, generally pear shaped, round which a rope eye may be spliced.
TWINE	Thin cord or line often used for whippings or seizings.
UNLAY	Separate the strands of a rope.
WHIPPING	A binding on the end of a rope to prevent it fraying.
WORKING END	The end of a rope or line with which a knot is tied.

1 OVERHAND KNOT

The **Overhand Knot** or **Thumb Knot** is the simplest of all knots. It's widely used and forms an integral part of many other knots, including **2**, **5**, **26**, **27**, **29** and **45** as examples. The Overhand Knot can be used as a temporary stopper knot (see *Glossary*) in the end of a line and is often tied in the end of string, twine and other small stuff to prevent the end unlaying and fraying. Such use is, however, considered unseaman-like. (See **50** and **51** for alternatives.)

2 HALF HITCH

The **Half Hitch** is rarely used on its own, but forms a basic component in many knots, including **30**, **34**, **39** and **40**.

3 SLIPPED HALF HITCH

The **Slipped Half Hitch** provides a quick-release facility where otherwise the ordinary half hitch would be used. 'Slipping' a knot in this way must be used with care to maintain the security of the knot, but is valuable. (See examples such as **7** and **8**).

4 FIGURE OF EIGHT KNOT

The **Figure of Eight Knot** is a better stopper knot than **1**, because it is bulkier and remains much easier to undo. It is the seaman's choice for a stopper knot.

5 REEF KNOT

The **Reef Knot** or **Square Knot** can be tied when there is tension on both parts. It is used to enclose or bind something – for example a bundle of sticks or a section of the sail when reefing. (Its first name comes from its use in reefing a sail; its second from its symmetrical shape.) The knot can slip if the two parts are of different dimensions or materials and can spill if one end is tugged sharply, especially if used with shiny, synthetic rope. For these reasons it should not be used as a bend to join two lines. The knot consists of two Overhand Knots (**1**) tied on top of each other with the second formed in the opposite direction to the first. This results in the ends lying neatly alongside the standing parts. Follow the pattern: left over right and tuck under, right over left and tuck under.

6 GRANNY KNOT

The **Granny Knot** or **Lubber's Knot** will either slip undone or jam tight. It should never be used and is recognized by the ends standing out rather than lying beside the standing parts.

7 SLIPPED REEF KNOT

The **Slipped Reef Knot** or **Draw Knot** is just a Reef Knot (**5**) with one working end formed into a loop through the centre of the knot. It has the advantage of being easy to untie.

8 DOUBLE SLIPPED REEF KNOT

The **Double Slipped Reef Knot** or **Bow Knot** is most commonly used for tying shoe laces, but is equally good for sail ties. The form is 'square' in the same way as a Reef Knot and it is easily undone by pulling on the ends.

9

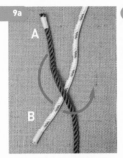

9 SHEET BEND

The **Sheet Bend** or **Weaver's Knot** offers a quick and easy way to join two ropes together, and is particularly useful if the ropes are of differing sizes. It holds well in most ropes, but may be doubled (see **11**) in particularly slippery ones.

To form the sheet bend, cross end **A** over **B** (**9a**) then bring **A** down behind **B** and up again in one twisting movement to form a loop (**C**) in rope **B**, with **A** coming up through it (**9b**). Now pass end **A** behind the standing part (**D**) of rope **B** and tuck it down through loop **C** parallel to its own standing part (**E**) (**9c**). Work the knot tight and it should look as in **9d** (front view) and **9e** (back view).

If the two lines being joined are of different diameters, make sure that the larger rope is rope **B**, so that most of the weaving is done by the thinner, more easily worked line **A**.

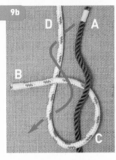

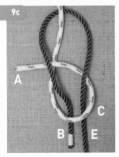

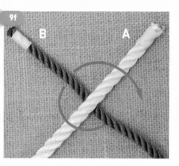

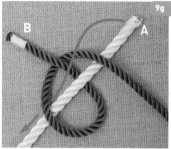

Weavers produce the same knot by a rather different method. They cross **A** over **B** (**9f**) then pass a bight of **B** around its own working end (**9g**). They then pass end **A** up across the standing part of **B** (follow the arrow in **9g**) and down through the loop in **B** (**9h**). The knot is then settled down and is just like that in **9d** and **9e**.

It may be slightly confusing that although both the Reef Knot and the Sheet Bend are used to tie the ends of rope together, one is called a knot and the other a bend. The distinction is probably due to the different functions performed by them. Mariners use the Sheet Bend to 'bend' one free line onto another free line, while they use the Reef Knot to 'tie' or 'knot' the two free ends of a single line round a bundle or some other object. Certainly the Reef Knot should never be used in place of a Sheet Bend.

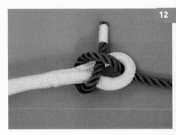

10 LEFT-HANDED SHEET BEND

It is possible for the **Left-Handed Sheet Bend**, in which the ends are on opposite sides to each other, to slip and so for that reason it is best avoided.

11 DOUBLE SHEET BEND

The **Double Sheet Bend** incorporates an extra binding turn and is generally stronger than the single form (**9**). It is particularly useful when bending a line to one of significantly larger diameter or one that is very stiff.

12 BECKET BEND

The **Becket Bend** is exactly the same as a Sheet Bend (**9**), but is so named when one rope has an eye (becket) formed in its end. Like the Sheet Bend, the Becket Bend can be doubled for security (**11**).

13 HEAVING LINE BEND

The **Heaving Line Bend** is used to attach a light heaving line to a heavier hawser or mooring warp that cannot easily be thrown ashore by itself. The heaving line is sent ashore and used to pull the hawser across, attached by the Heaving Line Bend.

14 CARRICK BEND

The **Carrick Bend** is strong, secure and pleasing to form with its regular, symmetrical woven pattern. It normally remains quite easy to pick apart after use.

When forming the bend, be sure to follow the regular over-and-under weaving pattern to end up with lines emerging opposite each other from all four corners (**14a**). Once formed, work the bend up tight and as it is settled it will capsize and form into a compact square with two clear loops

(**14b**) that can later be prised apart (with a marline spike if necessary) to loosen and untie. This characteristic of being easily undone makes the Carrick Bend particularly useful.

The Carrick Bend can also be used to form a practical door mat. With the bend laid out flat (**14a**), the parts are doubled or tripled and the ends cut off and tucked in securely. Do not tighten the bend so far that it capsizes, but leave it as a flat pattern.

15 BOWLINE BEND

The **Bowline Bend** is a simple and extremely useful way of joining two lines of similar or dissimilar diameter. It takes up a fair bit of rope and remains quite bulky, but it's secure, easily untied and reliable. It consists of two interlinking Bowlines (**20**) and is made even more secure if the ends are either secured to the loop with a seizing or with a Half Hitch (**2**).

16 STRAP KNOT

The **Strap Knot** is designed for joining
either leather straps or flat webbing
ones such as those used for strapping
dinghies onto trailers. It's not a knot
to be used in rope as it will either jam
or slip undone as soon as your back
is turned.

17 WATER KNOT

The **Water Knot** or **Tape Knot** is also
referred to as a Doubled Overhand
Knot, because it is formed by first
tying an Overhand Knot (**1**) as in **17a**
and then weaving the second line or
tape back through to double the knot
in the opposite direction (**17b-17d**).
The knot holds well in slippery
synthetics and is used widely by
climbers for joining webbing tapes.

18 HUNTER'S BEND

The **Hunter's Bend**, once known as the Rigger's Bend, is another good knot to use when joining slippery ropes together. The ends are laid together in opposite directions and twisted to form two loops as in **18a**.

One end is then brought forward and tucked back through the loop (**18b**) before the other is taken back and brought up through the loop (**18c**). The whole knot is then settled together and worked up tight (**18d**).

19 FIGURE OF EIGHT BEND

The **Figure of Eight Bend** is made up of two Figures of Eight (**4**) woven together in opposite directions. Begin by forming a figure of eight in one rope and pass the working end of the other rope up through the first loop (**19a**). Follow round the parts (**19b** and **19c**) until the original figure of eight is doubled. Finish by settling the knot (**19d**).

3 LOOPS

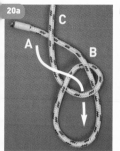

20 BOWLINE

The **Bowline** (rhymes with 'stolen') is the most useful way to form a fixed loop in the end of a rope or line. It is simple, quickly tied, strong and secure, and rarely slips or jams, even under heavy loading. The knot is formed (**20a**) by making a small, anti-clockwise loop (**B**), then passing the working end (**A**) up through it and continuing in an anti-clockwise direction behind the standing part (**C**) and back down through the small loop (**B**) so that the end lies parallel to the side of the main loop (**20b**).

Many people prefer to form the small initial loop with the working end poking up through it in one step. They do this by placing the end across on top of the standing part, holding the two together with their

right hand, and twisting with the fingers going downwards and up through the large loop. It's a knack, once learned, that allows the bowline to be tied with one hand.

20c shows a **Left-Handed** or **German Bowline** with the end on the outside of the main loop. This variant is no stronger than the normal Bowline, but can, in some circumstances, be a little more secure. It is most likely to be used when attaching sheets to the clew of a headsail. The argument in its favour is that when the sail flogs, the end of the sheet is less likely to be pushed back making the knot come undone. However, if this is a concern, a normal Bowline can be used with the end dogged to the side of the loop with a Half Hitch.

21 TOGGLE

A round or long **Toggle** is a simple way of joining the ends of two light lines that may have to be separated at just a moment's notice. The end without the Toggle needs an eye formed in it using a Bowline (**20**), an Eye Splice (**75**) or a Round Seizing (**52**).

22 BOWLINE ON THE BIGHT

The **Bowline on the Bight** is tied in the middle of a line when a loop is needed, but both ends are inaccessible. The load should be applied equally to both standing loops. It makes a good sling or (uncomfortable) emergency bosun's chair.

It is formed initially just like a normal Bowline (**20**) to produce a small anti-clockwise loop (**A**) with the bight (**B**) poking up through it (**22a**). The bight (**B**) is then enlarged so that it can be spread out and dropped down over the main loop (**C**) (**22b**). The bight (**B**) is then passed up behind the main loop (**C**) to settle against the two standing parts of the line (**22c**).

23 PORTUGUESE BOWLINE

The **Portuguese Bowline**, like the Bowline on the Bight (**22**), provides a pair of loops, but in this case it is tied at the end of a line and the two loops can be adjusted for size. This is useful when using the Portuguese Bowline as a temporary bosun's chair, because one loop can be sat in while the other is adjusted for size and drawn up to support the person's back with the knot itself against his or her chest.

To tie the Portuguese Bowline first form a small anti-clockwise loop, then pass the working end up through it. Form a second anti-clockwise loop and again pass the working end up through the small loop (**23a**). Finish by passing the working end behind the standing part, in an anti-clockwise direction, and down through the small loop (**23b**). The two loops can now be adjusted separately for size (**23c**).

24 SPANISH BOWLINE

The **Spanish Bowline** provides two adjustable loops, which may be used to support a plank or ladder when used as a horizontal painting platform, or as an emergency bosun's chair, with one of the occupant's legs in each loop. This would not be ideal as it provides no back support and would have to be used with great caution.

Start the Spanish Bowline by forming three loops as shown in **24a**, taking careful note of their direction of formation. Keep the centre loop rather larger than the outside ones. Fold that larger middle loop forwards and down over the two smaller loops

as shown in **24b**, then enlarge it, if necessary, so that it encircles the two smaller loops as in **24c**. Now pull the sides of the big loop up through the two smaller loops to form 'ears', as shown in **24d**. These 'ears' can now be adjusted by working the required line through the knot before tightening everything up securely.

Notice that the lower edge of the large loop (now the 'ears') is free to slide back and forth through the heart of the knot. This makes the ear loops adjustable in size with respect to each other – either intentionally or unintentionally. Beware of the latter.

25 RUNNING BOWLINE

The **Running Bowline** consists of a Bowline (**20**) formed with a very small loop tied round the standing part. It provides a secure and useful temporary noose or running knot.

26 OVERHAND RUNNING KNOT

The **Overhand Running Knot** or **Noose** is the simplest of several temporary running knots or slip knots and is formed using a simple Overhand or Thumb Knot (**1**). To tie it, form a loop as in **26a** and use your fingers (pushed down through the loop) to draw a bight of the standing part up through the loop. By doing so, an Overhand Knot will be formed around the standing part, as shown in **26b**. Draw the Overhand Knot tight and adjust the loop to the size required.

27 OVERHAND LOOP

The **Overhand Loop** or **Loop Knot** is the simplest way to tie a fixed loop in the end of a piece of cord or light line. It should not be used in rope, however, because it tends to jam and cannot be readily undone. Knots tied in rope, which is expensive, generally need to be untied when they have served their purpose, so that the rope is ready for further use. Knots tied in cord or light line can, if necessary, be cut off and discarded when they have been used. Hence a knot that is appropriate in one material is sometimes quite inappropriate in another material or size of line. For rope, a better knot to use would be the Figure of Eight Loop (**28**).

The Overhand Loop is very unlikely to shake loose and become untied, but the Bowline (**20**), which is structurally a better knot, can, particularly when formed in rope made of a slippery material. When there is danger of it doing so, the end of a Bowline should always be stopped (*see Glossary*) to the standing part or secured to it with an Overhand Knot [**1**] or Half Hitch [**2**].

To form the Overhand Loop, just make a loop and tie an Overhand Knot (**1**) using the two parts together.

28 FIGURE OF EIGHT LOOP

The **Figure of Eight Loop** is a more seamanlike knot than the Overhand Loop (**27**) and is also used extensively by climbers. It is a little easier to loosen and untie than an Overhand Loop that has been heavily loaded. It is tied quite simply by forming a long loop in the end of a line and tying a Figure of Eight (**4**) in the doubled standing part.

29 FISHERMAN'S LOOP

The **Fisherman's Loop, Englishman's Loop** or **True-Lover's Loop** is hardly a sailor's knot, but is well known to fishermen. It looks strong, but can have a low breaking strength. However, it is often used in light lines or filaments.

To tie it, form two Overlapping Loops (**29a**) and draw the upper part **A** down and out through the centre **B**. The finished knot, when settled down (**29b**), has two Overhand Knots that lie snugly together and cannot slip (hence, perhaps, the True-Lover's name). Like many other knots, this is just one method of tying the knot, but it has the benefit of few steps.

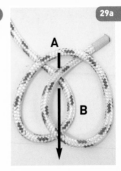

30 TAUTLINE HITCH

The Tautline Hitch, which gets its name from being used to adjust the guy ropes on tents, is made up of a Rolling Hitch (**42**) formed with the working end of a line applied to its own standing part. The hitch can be moved up to tighten the line, but then, when loaded, it holds firmly, providing a taut line. Start by forming a loop (**30a**) and roll the working end down round the standing part into the loop. Then take the working end up and apply a Half Hitch (**2**) above the starting point (**30b**). The hitch is then worked tight (**30c**) and the loop adjusted and loaded.

31 MANHARNESS KNOT

The **Manharness Knot** enables you to form a secure loop in a line whose ends are fixed, and a sequence of Manharness Knots can actually be used to make a rudimentary ladder in an emergency. Beware though, because if yanked out of shape the knot is likely to turn into a running knot or noose. The Butterfly Knot [**63**] may be a better knot for this purpose.

Begin by forming a loop as in **31a**, then weave the lower side of the loop under the crossing line and over the upper side of the loop to achieve the shape in **31b**. From there it is simply a case of adjusting the loop size and then settling the knot securely, as in **31c**.

32a

32 MIDSHIPMAN'S HITCH

The **Midshipman's Hitch** provides a strong, secure loop. The hitch is based on the Rolling Hitch (**42**), which will not jam when loaded. Interestingly, it has been used by people in the water who have been thrown a rescue line to pull them back to the boat or shore. They have reached the stage shown in **32c** and then held the end against the standing part of the line above the hitch. This has proved sufficient for their rescue.

To form the Midshipman's Hitch, start by forming a loop and tucking the working end under the standing part as shown in **32a**. Then turn the working end around the loop and standing part together as in **32b**. Send the working end up to cross the standing part above the loop (**32c**) before forming an inward Half Hitch around the standing part as in **32d**. A Rolling Hitch has now been formed around the standing part and can be settled and loaded (**32e**). In slippery synthetic line there may be some initial slippage, but with the hitch worked tight it will soon hold securely.

32b

32c

32d

32e

33 TARBUCK KNOT

The **Tarbuck Knot**, like the Midshipman's Hitch (**32**), provides a secure loop. It is a little more complicated to form, but is well suited to modern synthetic ropes and is often used by climbers.

Start by forming a loop with the working end tucked up through it (**33a**). Take another turn around and down the side of the loop (**33b**) before leading the working end up over the round turns to pass behind the standing part (**33c**). Finish by tucking the working end across and under in a Figure of Eight pattern as in **33d**. Work the knot tight and apply load (**33e**). As with the Midshipman's Hitch, there may be a little slippage initially, but it will quickly grip and hold securely.

34 BUNTLINE HITCH

The **Buntline Hitch** produces a sliding loop that was originally used to secure the buntlines to the foot of a sail on square rigged ships. It consists of an inward-formed Clove Hitch (**41**) about the standing part and, because the second Half Hitch is nipped inside the first when the knot is drawn tight, it is a very secure hitch – it needed to be to withstand the flogging of the sail.

35 CATSPAW

The **Catspaw** is used to hitch a sling to a hook. It is formed by twisting two loops and then slipping them onto the hook. Begin by taking a bight of the sling and folding it down to make two loops as in **35a**. Next twist the two loops outwards (**35b**) several times before slipping the hook into place (**35c**). The Catspaw cannot jam – it actually falls apart as soon as the hook is taken away – and works best with an even pull on the two standing parts.

36 SHEEPSHANK

The **Sheepshank** is a rarely used, but potentially very useful knot indeed. It has the effect of shortening a rope and is commonly regarded as being for that purpose, but its real importance is in providing a way of bypassing an area of damage in a line. It will fall apart unless tension is maintained on the two ends, but while that is done, the section of line across the middle can actually be cut right through and the sheepshank will remain intact. This makes it possible to use a chafed line until it can be renewed. If that will not be for some time, then additional security can be created by seizing the two 'ears' to their respective standing parts.

37 LARK'S HEAD or COW HITCH

The **Lark's Head** or **Cow Hitch** is a good knot to use when the load will be carried on both parts. It is used most commonly to attach baggage tags or key labels and is structurally the same as the Bale Sling (**73**).

38 TWO HALF HITCHES

Two Half Hitches can be used to hitch a line temporarily to a ring, post or dockside loop. The two hitches are put on in the same direction (**38a**) so that, when worked tight, they form a Clove Hitch (**41**) about the standing part (**38b**).

39 ROUND TURN AND TWO HALF HITCHES

The **Round Turn and Two Half Hitches** is clearly similar to **38**, but with the significant difference that an initial full turn is taken (**39a**) before applying the two Half Hitches to form the complete knot (**39b**). The initial round turn gives a surprising degree of extra security to the hitch and makes it widely useful as well as very practical on board boats. It is, for example, the best way to tie on fenders when berthing alongside.

40 FISHERMAN'S BEND

The **Fisherman's Bend** or **Anchor Bend** is similar to a Round Turn and Two Half Hitches (**39**), but has a trapped turn against the ring or spar to give it added security. If it's left in place over any length of time a careful watch must be kept for chafe, because damage to the trapped part would undermine the integrity of the bend. **40a** shows the round turn and trapped part, while **40b** shows the second Half Hitch in place. Some people like to seize the end against the standing part as a 'belt and braces' measure.

41 CLOVE HITCH

The **Clove Hitch** or **Ratline Hitch** is one of the most misused knots or hitches. It is often used, for example, to secure a fender rope to a guard-wire, which is wrong, because there will be load on only one end and the hitch will eventually roll undone and the fender will be lost overboard. (Fenders should not, in any case, be tied to guardwires. The way to hang fenders is by using a Round Turn and Two Half Hitches (**39**) from a stanchion base or toerail.)

The point of a Clove Hitch is to secure a line to a mid-point. This might be setting up ratlines across shrouds (hence the alternative name) or securing the tiller while at anchor. The requirement is always for a load on each end of the line.

There are two ways to form the hitch. One is by rolling the line around a spar (or fixed point) as shown in **41a-c**, and the other is by dropping loops over the open end of a tiller, spar or post as in **41d-f**. The result is the same in each case.

The **Rolling Hitch** or **Stopper Hitch** is used to secure a smaller line to a larger one or to a spar when the load on the smaller line will be parallel to or nearly parallel to the larger line or spar. The hitch is formed a little differently about a rope and about a spar.

To form the Rolling Hitch about a rope, first determine the direction of the load, then apply turns as in **42a** and **42b** away from the load and so that the turns trap the load-bearing part of the line against the larger rope. After the second turn, lead the line above the load-bearing part and apply a Half Hitch around the larger rope (**42c** and **42d**). Settle the hitch down and apply load to it (**42e**) so that the pull is against the binding turns.

When securing a line to a spar or mooring post (**42f**), begin again by determining the direction of pull, but then apply the first couple of turns down the spar towards the load. Finally cross the line

over the turns and apply a Half Hitch above the load point. Should there be any doubt about the holding power of this hitch, whether because of a slippery rope or a polished post, extra initial turns can be applied and a second Half Hitch added.

43 STUDDINGSAIL HALYARD BEND

The **Studdingsail Halyard Bend** (pronounced 'stuns'l') is formed just like a Fisherman's Bend (**40**), but instead of finishing with a Half Hitch, the working end is crossed over and tucked back under the first turn to trap it. This makes the bend secure, but leaves it easy to undo.

44 TOPSAIL HALYARD BEND

The **Topsail Halyard Bend** is very like the Fisherman's Bend (**40**) and the Studdingsail Halyard Bend (**43**). It incorporates an extra turn about the spar, but has the working end trapped under the first turn in just the same way. The added turn helps with ropes made from slippery materials.

45 TOM FOOL KNOT

The **Tom Fool Knot** is just a trick knot without any practical application, but is fun for children to play with. It is formed by making two loops (**45a**) and using them to tie an Overhand Knot (**1**) to result in **45b**.

46 SINGLE JUG SLING

The **Single Jug Sling** or **Rope Handcuffs** may be used for carrying or hoisting a jug or bottle aboard, or for securing a prisoner's hands. Begin by forming two overlapping loops (**46a**), exactly as you would to form a Clove Hitch (**41**) over the open end of a post, with the right-hand one on top of the left. (If the right-hand loop is placed under the left, the result will be a Tom Fool Knot.) Draw the two overlapping parts **B** and **C** out through the larger loops, with **C** coming out over **D** and **B** out beneath **A** to produce the knot in **46b**.

To use the knot to lift or carry a jug or bottle, place the neck of the bottle in the centre of the knot, tighten it, then tie the ends together with a Reef Knot (**5**) and lift with the two loops.

For handcuffs, place the prisoner's hands in the two loops, pull on the ends to tighten the loops around the wrists and tie the ends together with a Reef Knot.

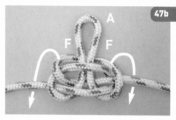

47 JUG SLING

The **Jug Sling** or **Hackamore**. Lay down two loops as in **47a**, with the right-hand one on top of the left. Weave bight **A** up under part **B**, pass it over part **C** and up under part **D** to emerge over part **E** (**47b**).

Next fold the loop **F** back and down, as shown by the arrows in **47b** to lie below the knot against the two standing parts. Now fold loop **G** forwards and down, as shown by the arrow in **47c** until it lies below the knot against the two standing parts (**47d**). Fit the neck of the jar or bottle into the centre of the knot, adjust the parts snugly, and join the two ends together in a loop with a Reef Knot (**5**). Carry the bottle using the loop handle **H** and the loop formed by the ends that you've just tied together.

This is an astonishingly secure and ingenious knot. It will lift the heaviest and most slippery of bottles, even if the rim or flange is almost imperceptible. In the American West it goes under the name Hackamore, and is said to be used as a temporary rope bridle. The knot appears to have been known to the ancient Greeks and Romans and, as usual, there are several different methods of tying it.

48 JURY KNOT

The **Jury Knot** or **Masthead Knot** is designed to be fitted to the head of a jury (emergency or temporary) mast, providing four attachment points for shrouds (supporting lines). To form the knot, begin by laying out three loops (**48a**) with each formed in the same direction. Overlap the right hand loop onto the middle one and that one onto the left hand loop. Then cross the two middle bights (**48b**) left over right, and weave them, over and under, out to the sides. Pull them out as side loops and pull the centre loop up (**48c**). By joining the free ends together there are now four loops to bend shrouds to with double Becket Bends (**12**) as in **48d**. The Masthead Knot is also useful for rigging a mast in a yacht's tender.

5 BELAYING OR CLEATING

49 BELAYING OR CLEATING

The term 'belaying' or 'cleating' means making
a line fast by winding it in figure of eight patterns
around the horns of a cleat. In days past the cleat
might have been a belaying pin or a pair of bitts,
but these are rare sights on a modern boat.

A cleat should, correctly, be angled to provide
a fair lead to the incoming line, which should be
led in to the back of the cleat (**49a**). Unfortunately
most boats these days have their cleats set in line
not at an angle. It may well be argued that a full
round turn should be taken initially, rather than the
turn shown here, but rope size and the length of
the horns on the cleat may preclude it. In either
case, now begin to follow a figure of eight pattern
round the horns (**49b** and **49c**). Two or three
patterns should be sufficient for a good grip.
Some people like to put on a locking turn, but it
is unnecessary if the horns are long enough to
prevent the figures of eight falling off. Where there
is any concern, form the locking turn in the same
way as the figures of eight (**49d**) and not against
the pattern as in **49e**.

50 COMMON WHIPPING

The **Common Whipping** or **Plain Whipping**, as both its names imply, is a simple, basic way of preventing a rope's end from fraying. It may, of course, be heat-sealed, but a whipping is more durable and the edges of a heat-sealed rope can be very sharp and painful on the hands.

To make any whipping, use a waxed whipping twine, which will grip well on the rope and itself. The large size of cord shown here is simply to improve clarity.

Start with a loop of twine laid towards the end of the rope (**50a**) and cover it with tight turns against the lay of the rope. Leave a short length of the loop clear of the turns and pass the whipping twine through it (**50b**). Draw the loop and the twine down under the seizing turns (**50c**) and trim the ends off short.

The finished whipping (**50d**) is neat and, if tight, will not enlarge the rope, so it will render easily through a block, fairlead or jammer.

51 WEST COUNTRY WHIPPING

The **West Country Whipping** is another quick and easy way to secure the end of a rope against fraying. It consists of a series of Overhand Knots (**1**) tied on opposite sides of the rope. First tie the twine around the rope (**51a**), then turn the rope over and tie the next Overhand Knot (**51b**). Turn back again and make another knot, then turn over and repeat as far as is required (**51c**) before finishing with a Reef Knot (**5**).

If the rope being whipped is at all hard, the West Country Whipping will enlarge it. Check that it will still render through fairleads or jammers if required to.

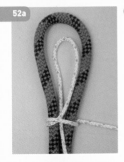

52 ROUND SEIZING

The **Round Seizing** is akin to a Common Whipping (**50**), but is usually used to bind two parts of a rope together. It is begun like the Common Whipping by laying a loop of whipping twine or light cord (depending upon the size of the rope being seized) towards the eye as in **52a**. Next lay on a series of binding turns and pass the end of the whipping twine or cord through the enclosed loop (**52b**). Draw the loop down to the top of the seizing (**52c**) then pass the working end of the twine round the seizing turns, between the two parts of the rope, in a series of tight turns. Finish off (**52d**) by tying the two ends of the seizing together with a Reef Knot (**5**) between the two parts of the rope.

(Remember that when using whipping twine it will look far smaller and neater than it does in this photo where cord is used for clarity.)

53 RACKING SEIZING

The **Racking Seizing** is used in preference to a Round Seizing (**52**) when more load will be placed on one of the seized parts than the other, such as when forming an eye in the end of a line. Depending upon the size of rope being seized, a single run of Racked Seizing can be put on (as shown here) or a double run can be used with the turns of the second layer fitting between those of the first. With heavy ropes, where cord is used for the seizing, the turns can be hove taut with a Marline Spike Hitch (**54**).

On most normal sizes of boat ropes a single layer of seizing will be sufficient. Begin by securing the seizing twine or cord to one part of the rope using a Clove Hitch (**41**). Weave the seizing on in a series of figures of eight around the two parts of the rope (**53a**) and close them up tight (**53b**). Next apply a series of binding turns between the two rope parts to tighten the whole seizing (**53c**), before finishing by tying the two ends of the seizing together with a Reef Knot (**5**) as shown in **53d**. Here it has been placed outside for clarity, but for security it is best placed between the two rope parts.

54 MARLINE SPIKE HITCH

The **Marline Spike Hitch** can be tied quickly and released instantly, just by withdrawing the marline spike or bar. It is an excellent way of gaining a good pulling grip on a rope or line that is otherwise hard to grip. Always pull against the crossed part (**A**); don't put the load on that side.

Form a crossed loop as in **54a**, with the load-bearing part of the line entering from top left in the photo. Slip a marline spike or stout bar under the loaded part and across the loop (**54b**), then pull against the crossed part (**A**).

8 END OR STOPPER KNOTS

55 DOUBLE FIGURE OF EIGHT

The **Double Figure of Eight** is a Figure of Eight Knot (**4**) with an extra twist put in. Begin as if to form a Figure of Eight (**55a**), but instead of passing the end straight down through the lower loop, instead pass it behind and up

through the loop (**55b**). Then settle the knot down as shown in **55c**. This knot is just as simple as the ordinary Figure of Eight but has greater bulk to stop a line running out through a block or eye.

56 CROWN KNOT

The **Crown Knot** is never used alone, but always forms part of another knot. Begin by putting a tape stopper around the rope and unlaying it to that point. Use tape to whip the ends

of each of the three strands, then tuck each down over its neighbour, working around in the direction of the lay (**56a**). Carefully tighten the knot until it forms as in **56b** then **56c**.

57 WALL KNOT

The **Wall Knot** is exactly the reverse of the Crown Knot (**56**). Where each strand in the crown is tucked downwards, in the Wall Knot it is tucked upwards. Start by putting a tape whipping on the rope and unlay the strands to it, then use tape to whip the end of each strand. In the direction of the lay of the rope, tuck each strand up under its neighbour in the pattern shown in **57a**. Gently work them all tight until they are settled as in **57b**. All that remains is to re-lay the rope so that the wall knot sits within a fully laid section of rope (**57c**) and whip the end. This provides an attractive stopper knot, but without too much bulk.

58 DOUBLE WALL KNOT

The **Double Wall Knot** is a bulkier knot than its single version (**57**) but is no harder to form. Put a tape whipping round the rope, unlay the three strands to that point and tape their ends. Tuck each strand up under its neighbour in the same direction as the lay and then repeat, so that the pattern is doubled. Work the knot tight, re-lay the strands together and whip the end for a neat finish (**58**).

59 MANROPE KNOT

The **Manrope Knot** or **Double Wall and Crown Knot** makes use of both the Double Wall Knot (**58**) and the Crown Knot (**56**) – just as the name suggests – to form a large stopper knot that used to be used in the end of a rope provided to help you haul yourself aboard. The Double Wall Knot is tied first with the Crown Knot above it.

Begin the Double Wall Knot by tucking each strand up under its neighbour in a pattern following the direction of the rope's lay (**59a**). Leave everything very loose at this stage. Next form a Crown Knot by tucking each strand down over its neighbour in the same direction as the lay (**59b**), again keeping all the strands loose. Now, with each knot formed, lead the strands down and follow round the Wall Knot to double it (**59c** and **59d**). Finally double round the Crown Knot and gently work the whole knot tight (**59e**) before cutting off the strands close under the finished knot and tucking them out of sight.

60 TURK'S HEAD

The **Turk's Head** is just one of many decorative knots that were once widely used by seamen who 'made tiddly' their ships and boats during the long watches of a deep sea voyage. They are a study in them-selves and there are many larger books that delve far deeper into the subject than is possible in a pocket book like this. However, any decora-tion makes a boat look loved and cared for, and the Turk's Head is ideal for smartening up a boat while also serving a practical purpose, such as giving extra grip on a tiller or marking the centred position on a wheel.

First form a Clove Hitch (**41**) loosely about the tiller or wheel (**60a** and **60b**). Turn the hitch over and cross the two parts over (**60c**). If the Clove Hitch was formed in the same direction as shown here, then the right-hand part should be crossed over the left. Next tuck the working end inwards under the recently crossed right-hand part (**60d**). Pass the working end over and inwards under the next part (**60e**). Pass it over one more time and inwards

again (**60f**) then the end begins
to double the knot.

Follow the pattern round to
double it, completing the Turk's Head
as in **60g** by cutting the ends off short
and tucking them in. This shows the
knot doubled, but it can be tripled
if preferred.

10 TO WEIGHT A HEAVING LINE

61 MONKEY'S FIST

The **Monkey's Fist** is the knot of
traditional choice for weighting the
end of a heaving line. In most
instances it is heavy enough on
its own to carry a light line a long way
when thrown, but occasionally the fist
is given greater weight by including a
stone or other weight in its centre. If
that is done, the heaving line must be
used with particular care to avoid
injuring anyone.

   To begin the fist, form three turns
(**61a**) before turning the line at right
angles and circling the first loops

three times (**61b**). Next turn at right
angles again and circle the second
set of loops (**61c**) by passing the line
round inside the first (original) set
of loops. At that point the fist is
completed, but needs to be worked
tight (and a weight put in if really
needed) so that it ends up as in **61d**.
If it's made in three strand line the
end can be spliced into the standing
part, but if it is made with braided
rope the end can be seized (**52**) to the
standing part.

62 SURGEON'S KNOT

The **Surgeon's Knot** or **Ligature Knot** comes from tying slippery sutures and is a smart and secure way of tying any slippery synthetic line more securely than a Reef Knot (**5**). The knot is begun by making an Overhand Knot (**1**) with an extra turn, as in **62a**. Then, taking care to keep the ends on their own sides, tie another Overhand Knot (**62b**) in the opposite direction. That's the knot; it now needs only to be tightened until it settles neatly into the shape shown in **62c**.

A variation on the Surgeon's Knot is formed by making an Overhand Knot with the extra turn, followed by a second Overhand Knot with an extra turn to give the shape shown in **62d**.

63 BUTTERFLY KNOT

The **Butterfly Knot** is a good one to use for a temporary harness in the middle of a line. It won't pull out of shape and become a slip noose, nor will it jam, and it is easily undone even after loading. It can also be hauled on from either direction and still remain intact.

The knot is formed by laying down two overlapping right hand loops, one encompassing the other (**63a**). Lift the upper part of the inner loop over the crossover and then lead it back and up through itself and the larger loop to form the shape in **63b**. Now settle and tighten the knot, adjusting the loop as necessary (**63c**).

The **Constrictor Knot** makes an extremely useful temporary whipping or seizing and will hold pieces of wood together while being glued. It is therefore useful for a wide range of household repairs. Each time the knot is pulled tighter it just holds harder, without any slippage. However, this does make it hard to untie after use.

Begin as if making a Clove Hitch (**41**) as in **64a**, but cross the working part over and tuck it under the two parts on the right as in **64b**. Then pull tight (**64c**).

65 STANLEY BARNES KNOT

The **Stanley Barnes Knot** comes from the world of fishing. It is similar to a Figure of Eight Loop [**28**] but incorporates an extra twist for added security in nylon casts, leaders or spinning lines. It is strong, safe, easy to remember, streamlined and is well-suited to boat ropes.

Take a long bight of the line and lay out a figure of eight as in **65a**, then cross the bight over (**65b**) and bring it up through the main loop (**65c**). Now settle and tighten the knot adjusting the loop size as necessary (**65d**).

65b

65c

65d

66 BLOOD KNOT

The **Blood Knot** or **Barrel Knot** is an excellent way of tying the ends of two nylon casts or leaders together, or indeed any two small, slippery lines of roughly equal diameter.

Form the knot by laying the two ends parallel to each other, pointing in opposite directions and with a good overlap. Working from the outside inwards, use the end of each line to put two or three turns on to bind the two standing parts together (**66a**). Tuck the ends through between the standing parts in opposite directions. Now carefully tighten all the turns and pull the knot together until it settles and binds securely together as shown in **66b**.

67 PERFECT KNOT

The **Perfect Knot** has a lot to live up to in its name, but it is a well tried and proven knot for tying a nylon cast to a swivel. Pass the end of the line through the eye of the swivel and wrap it several times around the stem before passing it back through the eye in the opposite direction (**67a**). Leave the turns loose and lift them over the eye in order, beginning with the one furthest from the eye. Settle each above the eye, finishing with the one that was nearest to the eye again resting next to it, then tighten the knot as in **67b**.

68a

The **Prusik Knot** comes from the world of climbing and was devised by Dr Carl Prusik in 1931. It is used to attach a sling of either rope or climbing tape to a static line. The knot will slide along the static line, but then locks under load applied at an acute angle to the line. This means that with a pair of slings attached by Prusik Knots, a climber can ascend the static line.

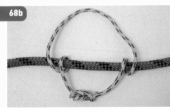

68b

Loop the sling – here a line with the ends joined by a Surgeon's Knot (**62**) – around the static line (**68a**) and pass the larger, outer loop several times around the smaller loop and static line (**68b**) in an outwards direction (**68c**). Send the smaller loop through the larger one (**68d**) and work the knot tight, enlarging what was the smaller loop. Now the knot can be slipped along the line, but will hold securely if a load is put on at an angle (**68e**).

68c

68d

68e

69 KLEMHEIST KNOT

The **Klemheist Knot** is very similar to the Prusik Knot (**68**). It is used to attach a sling to a static line and will jam when loaded at an acute angle.

Wrap the sling around the static line three or four times (**69a**), then bring the loops together and pass one through the other (**69b**). Now settle the knot down, move to the required position and apply load (**69c**), ensuring that it is directed to pull against the short loop.

In this sense the Klemheist Knot differs from the Prusik Knot, because it can only be loaded successfully in one direction, whereas the Prusik will lock when loaded in either direction.

70 SPANISH WINDLASS

The **Spanish Windlass** has had many uses over the centuries. In the days of square riggers it would have been used to heave heavy hawsers together to apply a seizing, but with modern lightweight lines this use has disappeared. Instead it can now be very helpful in clearing a riding turn from a sheet winch or hauling in an anchor rode against a strong wind where it performs like a temporary windlass.

To haul on a line, whether an anchor rode or to relieve a sheet, turn the hauling rope around a sturdy bar supported securely at both ends. Insert a strong bar as in **70** and use that as a lever to roll around the bar. Depending on the length of the bar, a lot of power can be exerted.

The **Marling Hitch** is used for lacing a sail to a spar or dodgers (weather cloths) to a guardwire. It consists of a series of Half Hitches (**2**). 'To marl' means to secure with Marling Hitches.

Form it by tying a Half Hitch – like an Overhand Knot (**1**) but enclosing something – ie tying it around the spar or wire (**71a**) and repeat (**71b**) to form a chain (**71c**).

Take care to form a Half Hitch and not just a loop. As shown here, pass the working end down and forwards. Imagine pulling the spar out. You should be left with a series of knots (Overhand Knots). If you've not formed them correctly the loops would just fall apart.

The **Selvagee** is a way of attaching a sling or strop to a heavier line or spar to attach a hook, shackle or block. Wrap the strop around the line or spar (**72a**) and cross it over. Continue wrapping and crossing as far as its length will allow, then slip in the hook or shackle (**72b**).

73 BALE SLING

The **Bale Sling** uses a long Bowline (**20**) to form a Cow Hitch or Lark's Head (**37**) around a barrel, jug, water carrier, kit bag or whatever is to be lifted.

74 BARREL SLING

The **Barrel Sling** is a lifting knot for awkwardly shaped items. Stand the object on the lifting line some distance from its end and tie an Overhand Knot (**1**) over the top of the object (a jug in this photo). Spread the parts of the Overhand Knot out and settle them around the upper part of the jug, then join the working end to the standing part above the jug using a Bowline (**20**). Settle the knot and lift.

12 SPLICING

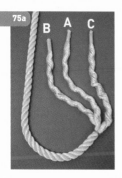

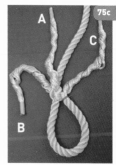

75 THREE STRAND EYE SPLICE

The **Three Strand Eye Splice** produces a completely secure and very strong eye in the end of a three strand laid rope. By weaving the individual strands back into the lay of the rope each is held tightly and the splice is neater than a knot. Unlike a knot, however, it cannot be readily untied.

Place a twine or tape seizing around the rope a good distance from the end and unlay the strands to it. Tape the end of each strand to prevent it fraying and to make tucking it into the rope easier (**75a**). Form an eye of the required size and tuck the middle strand **A** under one strand of the rope at the throat of the required eye (**75b**). Note that it is tucked against the direction of the rope's lay. This must be done with all of the tucks. Tuck the second strand **B** under the next strand round at the same level (**75c**), then turn the work over and tuck the third strand **C** under the remaining strand at the same level (**75d**).

Tuck each strand over and under a second time, working against the lay and tucking each strand at the same level. Then use each strand to put in a third tuck (**75e**). This should be a sufficient number of tucks, but if the ends of the strands are long enough, a fourth tuck would not hurt.

Settle the splice by gently rolling it under foot on a hard surface and giving it a good tug (**75f**). The ends of the strands can be cut off close or left loose. Trimming them short is, of course, neater, but is best done after a fourth tuck in case they slip back.

The strands can be halved before the fourth tuck to give a tapered finish if preferred, but beware – nylon will spring apart and be difficult to tuck as soon as the tape is removed from the end of the strand.

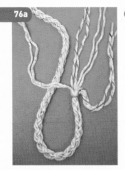
76a

76 MULTIPLAIT EYE SPLICE

The **Multiplait Eye Splice**, like the Three Strand Eye Splice (**75**) puts a totally secure eye in the end of a mooring or anchor warp, which is what multiplait is intended to be used for.

First note that multiplait is made up from four pairs of strands. Two of the pairs have a heavy black thread running through them and the other pair either has a fine black thread or none at all. Recognizing this difference between the pairs helps to make the tucks correctly.

76b

Begin by putting a tight twine or tape seizing on the rope a good distance from the end and then unlay the strands to make eight separate ones, but keep them close to each other in their pairs. Tape whip the end of each strand to stop it from fraying (**76a**).

At the throat of the required eye, tuck one pair of plain strands under a pair of plain strands in the standing part, followed by a pair of marked strands under a pair of similarly marked strands (**76b**). Turn the work over and repeat with the other pairs of strands.

For the second and subsequent tucks, keep the

76c

76d

plain and marked strands matched, but work singly, so that instead of tucking a pair under a pair, tuck one strand under one strand in the pair then the other strand under the remaining one. This gives the whole splice a characteristic tidy plaited appearance (**76c**).

When sufficient tucks have been made, seize the ends of the strands to their neighbours across a strand of the rope (**76d**). This will prevent them from untucking.

77 SHORT SPLICE

The **Short Splice** is a very strong way to join two pieces of a three strand rope together permanently. Its one drawback is that it substantially increases the diameter of the rope, which may prevent it going through a block or fairlead.

Start by unlaying both ropes for a good distance – always give yourself plenty to work with – and tape whip

the end of each strand. 'Marry' the two ropes together so that their strands lie together as in **77a**. Cross the two that are together and tuck one under the next strand, working against the lay. Tuck each of the other two strands in the same way (**77b**) then put a light seizing round the rope to hold everything in place (**77c**). Continue tucking on one side

of the seizing (**77d**) until three or four rounds of tucks have been completed.

At this point the seizing can be removed so that the tucks into the other side can be made tight as in **77e**. Continue tucking to completion

and then roll the splice gently under foot on a firm surface to settle it (**77f**).

The ends of the strands may be cut off short after the splice has been settled, but some people prefer to leave them as shown in case they work out.

78 MULTIPLAIT TO CHAIN SPLICE

The **Multiplait to Chain Splice** is one of the most important splices in use today. It is used to join a multiplait rope anchor rode to the all important anchor chain. The splice will pass through a chain pipe and should also run over the gipsy of an anchor winch or windlass. The splice looks harder to put in than it actually is, but it requires far more tucks than most splices because the chain links have no 'give' and therefore offer reduced grip between them and the (slippery) rope strands. (The splice in the photograph is short for clarity.)

Separate the eight strands and tape whip their ends. Unlay the rope for a distance equal to at least 12 links of the chain and put a

temporary seizing round the rope to hold it together. Open the rope so that, as you look down on the end (**78a**) you see two pairs of strands with a heavy black thread in them and two pairs either with a light thread or none at all. Place the end against the last link of the chain (**78b**) and tuck each of the four strands with black threads in them through the first link as in **78c**, with each pair going in opposite directions. Tuck one strand through, then its opposite one, so that they lie like laced fingers – this is important for subsequent tucks. Now turn the chain 90 degrees and tuck the two pairs of unmarked strands through the next link (**78d**), again lacing them alternately as in **78c**.

Continue tucking in this way, making sure that each pair of strands led on to the next link by straddling the intervening one (**78e**). When the final tucks have been put in, seize the strand ends together across the chain link so that they will not untuck when running across the bow roller, through the chain pipe or over the windlass gipsy (**78f**).

INDEX